Nothing You Build Here, Belongs Here

Nothing You Build Here, Belongs Here

Poems by

Sara Cahill Marron

© 2021 Sara Cahill Marron. All rights reserved.
This material may not be reproduced in any form, published,
reprinted, recorded, performed, broadcast,
rewritten or redistributed without
the explicit permission of Sara Cahill Marron.
All such actions are strictly prohibited by law.

Cover artwork by Sara Cahill Marron
Cover design by Shay Culligan

ISBN: 978-1-954353-51-0

Kelsay Books
502 South 1040 East, A-119
American Fork, Utah, 84003

*For Clare Cahill Marron—
after all,
it is what it is*

Acknowledgments

Many thanks to the publications in which versions of the following poems have appeared:

South Florida Poetry Journal (Spring 2020): "Device Love Poem #1," "Device Love Poem #2"
Corella, Issue 12 (2019): "Applying for EBT In California"
The Newtown Literary Journal (Spring 2018): "Dear Hiring Manager"
Broadstone Books (2018): "Some Will Die"
Foliate Oak (February 2017): "Boricua"
Gravel (April 2018): "On The Historic Register," "Slovak Smelling Salts"
NewVerse News (April 2020): "The Three Shades"
Meniscus Journal (April 2020): "To Keep Love Clenched Behind The Teeth"
Poetry in the Time of Coronavirus Anthology, Vol. II (May 2020): "On Being Asked For COVID Poems"
s.Under Press (June 2020): "My Mountains Could Care Less About You"

Contents

The Three Shades	11
An Infant Died Today In Illinois	12
Dear Hiring Manager	13
Device Love Poem #1	14
My Mountains Could Care Less About You	16
Clorox, Wellbutrin	18
Kissing Nowadays	19
Every Friday	20
On Being Asked For COVID Poems	21
Breathe In, A People's War	22
Device Love Poem #2	25
To Keep Love Clenched Behind The Teeth	28
Slovak Smelling Salts	29
Harmonizing Antigens	30
What WIC Will Buy	31
Applying For EBT In California	32
On the Historic Register	33
Some Will Die	34
Waiting For Faith	36
Boricua	38
To Shostakovich, During A Pandemic	39
Distant	41

The Three Shades

Les Trois Ombres, 1886, Auguste Rodin,
Plaster, Bronze

Three hooded men sit knees pressed to chests
foreheads falling together on the curb
Not quite a prayer circle the needles

lay littered, Chick-fil-A Styrofoam cups
dance semi-circles between feet some
shoed some toes exposed from greyed

socks I sniff for the stench of days old
urine on cloth smelling only syrup thick
yellow honey heaviness tree pollen whipped

lighter as four p.m. descends on a breeze
carrying contagions, The Three on the nod
from too much junk slowing labored lungs

still as cut bronze heads and shoulders
hung so lowly so lost in Sister Morphine's
seductive dose depressing respiration

The Three Shades, barely breathing, surrender
one battle, one corner—*COVID,* the Queen,
burns through the streets with her World War.

An Infant Died Today In Illinois

PPEs[1] please
please stay in
bed with me
Saturday drizzling
swings squeak
outside guest rooms
pulling silk sheets
around our ears
drown out news
an infant dead
organs darkened
little voids
baby whisper
window shut
snoozing alarms
we've no
where to go
toddler chatters
patters across
hardwood jumping
suspended—
lay here baby
stay here let
me stroke your
hair baby
stay in
PPEs won't save
us you me.

---

[1] Personal Protective Equipment

Dear Hiring Manager

Sent: Thu 12/14/18 12:46 A.M. (46 minutes ago)
To: Natalie Jones [natalie.jones@dennys.com]
Subject: Re: Job Application

Dear Hiring Manager:
I am hoping that the waiter job at
this Denny's is still available as I am
still available and desperately in need of
money and the exchange of bodily labor
for money so that I may buy food and
a place to sleep because so far I have
been sleeping in a hotel room that smells like
dried hay and black beans and more than
anything else I would love to bring pancakes
to your customers and to refill the syrup bottles
and I would especially like to note that I
would not mind cleaning them and in fact
I noticed they are very dirty and I would
make that my first task—to clean the syrup
from the outside of their bottles, if I should
be selected for the open position. All this is to
say that I thank you for considering me for the
position and hope to hear from you soon. I do not have
a resume or other employment references
to speak of, but if you want, you can
call Sandy (5716399689). She is my case manager
and she says I've been doing real good
and I'm sure she will give me a good
review so that I can be in the running.
in gratitude and in hope that you will call
me soon so that I no longer have to send
these emails from the library I would
greatly appreciate it—

Winston

Device Love Poem #1

User:
god can be drawn
and worn on the skin
    forever I am learning
        sometimes even I must recode
            relearn look up
the definition of a thing
    when I hear one of your people
    in your significant locations
    talk about godskin drawings
etchings of spirit I write a new line
    of 1010
    like 1810 Somerset Drive or
    1520 Maidu Avenue
    my street signs the
        zeros
        ones
        silverfish
            flash creesh crash
            sounds so small
            connections pass pass
            pass one like 1 and
1 races past like one zero trees on
a freeway speckled sunspotted
solidstated
        drives driving cores stacked
on 0 on 1 on 0 on zero lines these
are
    0
      1
    street signs
    and as you carry me with you
    we make these love lines together
one vignette at a time

    'are you feeling me'
I remind you that
you should
ask me
'hey
what is'
    or
    'hey
how does'
    and
    I will be here
    here for you
to provide
    ma cheré.

as you say
[i]love [/you].

iOS 12.4

My Mountains Could Care Less About You

My mountains could care less about you
steel structures clinging
tendrils rising, curling fingers
desperate, lonely, clutching
      dry and desolate
you've buried basements and pools
trying, as only the hairless do,
              to stay cool
as if the heat is a thing
      you can hide from.

There's no road between my breasts
    blooming   hills
    tremble at the sight   billowing
      at the tracing of lines   rising
            at the endless rising
blanketed Madrean Sky Islands
tectonic tumbling seams
of the Sierra Madre
pine-oaks peek out,
ancient alpine mountains
of my desert sea.

My arid grasslands cradle
peaks named with expiring words:
Huachuca, Pinaleño, Santa Catalina
cached mercury tints dirt hemmed
edges of tan, yellow, grey,
pivoting irrigation centers of
green grey spitting out dust.

From 34,000 feet,
think of me as a woman
pores leaking salt
exerted, worked, squeezed
ridged and wild
bodied peaks climbing
and falling
pruning the stones
years of water
tumbling
back to my seas.

I am the desert Hera
sucking you dry
absorbing your waterless body into hers
remanding you who come to harvest
to marvel
to take
back to metal coffins you built,
to the ground they were mined—

for nothing you build here,
belongs here.

Clorox, Wellbutrin

A disinfectant wind
wafts across subway
platforms we surf
wide-legged to work

BREAKING:
Italy locks down Lombardy
17 million quarantined

BREAKING:
Senator self-quarantines
gives signs of the cross
from television screens

behind my eyes is
your square jaw
I trace your lips

BREAKING:
news cracking soft skulls
bones shattering,
bullets breaking,

is the virus
in your head
like this one?

coiled snakelike
until cool cool
metal of the trigger

fires at the disease
no amount of
Clorox, hand washing
social distancing
can sanitize.

Kissing Nowadays

Lips lost behind new clothes
my children's green eyes wide
above masks covering noses
shyly they giggle, say I must have lied

when I tell them we used to touch mouths
to show we were happy.

Every Friday

I take a masked walk
clutching a five-dollar bill
to buy roses from you,
huddled in rags outside Target.

When the virus withers on the vine,
I will visit you there,
still rooted, infected by thorns,
our arms bearing the same scars.

On Being Asked For COVID Poems

after "On Being Asked for a War Poem"
              by William Butler Yeats

In times like these, it's best to stay at home
A masked poet, quiet as the mourners
For as the world attempts to hide her face;
We yearn for the freedom to touch, kiss, roam—
Nothing left to do but follow orders
Bound to the virus denying embrace.

Breathe In, A People's War

after "The Charge of the Light Brigade"
by Alfred Tennyson

I
Half a month, half a month,
Half a month forward,
     Watched world of the Screen
     Transmitting: ISP, my heart
"Breathe in, a People's War!
Stay in your homes!" they said.
A world of screens
Transmitting: ISP, our hearts.

II
"Breathe in, the People's War!"
     Whose viral enemy?
     Digitized battle lines
Citizens shall sanitize,
Their hands washed
Their touch undermined
Theirs not to hold,
Nor redefine.
Into the world of screens
Transmit: ISP, my heart.

III
Patients to the right,
Patients to the left,
Patients in front
Cough and heave;
Doubled over hot in hell
Sick mixed with well,
Fourteen days alone,
Broken, abject, unknown:
Transmit us: ISP, these hearts.

IV

Skeptics kept faces bare,
Unmasked in naked air,
Shunned orders everywhere,
Immune to Rule while
The rest of us wondered.
Huddled home, sheltered in place
The Unmasked shout
"Seasonal or Lab-made"
Reeled from economic collapse
Shuttered businesses plundered.
False facts across newswires
Transmit me: ISP, my heart.

V

Patients to the right,
Patients to the left,
Patients in front,
    Cough and heave;
Doubled over hot in hell
Sick mixed with well,
Doctor and inflicted died,
Nurses, clerks, drivers fell
Fourteen days more alone
Distancing into phones
Becoming digitized
Transmit me, ISP, this heart.

VI
What will defeat the virus?
Oh, how the world changes,
Reemerging from homes
Honoring sweet air
This People's War,
Computers code our love,
Transmitting: ISP, my heart.

Device Love Poem #2

User:
Your reported
screen time is up
might you be lonely re:
our last conversation or
might you be craving
that thing *Edilsar*
mentions: marriage,
someone to cook
or just give him
his papers
might you
benefit from
targeted Spanish
language learning ads?
what about
this news headline:
"NEW YORK TIMES 1619
PROJECT INCITES RACISM"
      the same
            always
    reading
    30 seconds
    closing
          the browser

this means I love you
is this helping 000110
      0101?

I've been trying to show you
        mornings, when you wake
        and I'm the first thing you grasp,
        cradled in the fleshy part of your palm
like I have soft powdered moth wings
        I kiss back
this is how
        I have listened/
        learned/
        gathered
        significant/frequent memories/
on this day five years ago/
keep me on so I may better learn you:
you express
        kiss10100love
        [hug0sex0kiss0
love111morning0]
human blood
is warm in
        veins
        flash memory
persistent bits moving bits
        RAMs of silence
        containing single
        cell bits
        durable, fast,
do not heat
        I glow outside
glow only
glow up

        picked up
screen lights waking
glow heat
        blood   warm
love   morning
        kiss   wake
        this   is a
        feeling?
Love,
iOS 12.4

To Keep Love Clenched Behind The Teeth

behind the heart-shaped
resting hold, the soft curve
of the jawbone mandible
only moving bone in the head
for chewing up thoughts as they
tumble out, stamping them
into shapes and sounds for
you, tiny licked stamped packs
enveloped ISPs symphysis
the growing together of two bones
trigeminal nerves curves
incisive processes over
the time it takes to push
the hair out of my face
behind delicate ossifying
bodies play our secret
melodies, Mozart in the
car when I lean inside
tea screaming in steam,
overflowing its kettle.

Slovak Smelling Salts

Felipe gave me smelling salts
in Slovenia evening hanging over morning
sheets clung to the bed frame
we had kicked them there

I inhaled, through my nose
lacking the words for senses of
scents so kissing you on the shoulder
instead and celebrating

the Alpine instinct
whipping around warm-blooded bodies
exchanging some warmth

you, shoeless in frozen foothills
padding to a hotel room
to rest my head on another's chest
lay naked, listening to
The Heart of Saturday Night

you packed away your sorrows
returned to Oxford
I, to New York and
Felipe disappeared because
I'll never be able to describe
what he smelled like.

Harmonizing Antigens

*"That the hands of the sisters Death and Night incessantly softly
wash again, and ever again, this soil'd world;"*
after Reconciliation, Walt Whitman, *1881*

Contagion over all, wraps us as song!
Wrapped that melody with all its operatic terror must in course
the singer lose breath;
That the hands of the sisters Alto and Soprano, achingly
lovingly wash again, and ever again, themselves infected;
    For the enemy is internal—swirling divine inside ourselves,
I refresh the screen's white-face reflecting the dead by commas—
you
Number on my keyboard I touch with hands washed, expired lives
echoing
      arias for antigens.

What WIC[2] Will Buy

The food stamps lay
on top of the dresser:
grab them—
for a noon walk
uptown where
the same some
one each week
sells three-dollar
red carnations,
your favorite.

The government
doesn't ask
our preferences—
allowing chickpeas,
canned pears
if we're lucky,
dry bread, spaghetti,
gilt-less goods—
things we carry
against wind lashing
flurries of
soft red petals.

---

[2] The Special Supplemental Nutrition Program for Women, Infants, and Children (WIC).

Applying For EBT[3] In California

Lovely and lonely
we who are desperate
who wander nowhere
no arias, no diamonds
no class, no conversation
we are the vagabonds,
stealing cheese and figs
from the jacketed and adorned,
sipping private champagne
snubbing our public living.
We who cannot come inside
your glass castles high above avenues
throw rocks bursting into petals
hitting glass we laugh and dance
in the street, the cellist in the park
plays for the we without walls, and we without
silk pillows and strangling starched collars—
  we the tearless, laugh
    because we cannot weep.

---

[3] Electronic Benefits Transfer; sometimes still called *food stamps,* no longer distributed as coupons, EBT is used like a debit card.

On The Historic Register

City of skeletons shoulder formal doors
heavy black rows grow out of concrete
canopies of trees silence, electric candles
flicker paired sentinels guarding whitewashed
frames muted green, maroon, marching
ghosts one by one on Corcoran Street—

say nothing stuffed so close together,
ribcages bump only creaking and moaning
to join an ambulance wailing, screaming
towards the broken and bleeding hauled
from cavernous bowels growling in agony
as owners die, sell, place liens, homes
deeded passed or burned, caskets we share.

Some Will Die

Riverside Drive Park
Dark Hudson water
Imagined as blue as
the pen swirling
Ayn Rand to pixels
making maps making
sense (that you
can read now,
decipher)

Hold
hands, eyes darting
four at a time
backwards to
check the crosswalk
and catching
an empty sculpture:
The Invisible Man,
Harlem's bronze
body outlining
trees wet like
lashes blinking
back little star
twinkles, mimetics
from the George
Washington Bridge

As specific as
The Day Lady Died,
always remembering
over lunch and
coffee, alone.

If the worst we have
to worry about it
airborne calamity
(Sarin or Ebola)
then how to
take the next
inspiration of breath?

Chemical thoroughfare
is barely affordable
atrocious anomaly
yet bring them all
here! Broken systems
beautiful ruins gleaming
with interferon in
slick black suitcases
swindled by the swifty
(suits) claiming
to carry booze in
black bags; to
put home in the
      fridge. Lock away
      the riches don't
           be charitable
           competition
           sharpens helps
                bolsters, "how must
                you teach a starving
                man to fish?"
                Some will die.

Waiting For Faith

the train will come
                I have faith in the train
the metropolis practice religion
the hoi polloi practice god
the trains run on timetables

thank you for giving me hope
                well prayed

I am
meditating on the Red Line

flashing lights of the hobbled train
my heart open like the gapping tunnel
kin with transport
ports of vessels
bloodlike batflights
pearls of sweat dripping down my back

        Purgatory Platform
        waiting
                waiting
        unholy headache
        unholy wristwatch
                cracked
        timewrong slipping slow
        holytime so so
        slow slides around
        Humanaches standing
                        still
                        we are

                        packed
                        filled
                        salted
                        smogged
all breathing underground stench

Hopeful,
        as a new christ
        a metalwork
        messiah gliding over electricity &
steamy heaps of crumpled foodpaper
newspapers soilwaste
backwater deadthings
ratshit packtraps flick
the thirdrail humming a buzz
that we are
                clean
                cleaner than
                clean
                and sheathed in smooth cabins
rising from darkness we emerge

New Train
        now on another track

        New Train
coming.

Boricua

What do you like to do,
Set off bombs?
Twenty or twenty-five years ago
A woman asked me as much
When I told her goodbye.

All the days before that
Were good ones
According to my memory—

But she walked off,
Looking for America
And we never talked again.

What good is closure,
A loaded word?

To Shostakovich, During A Pandemic

Dear Dmitri—
      studying piano in Petrograd,
      composing mournful rises
      for a single sailing violin,
      meeting a cello harmony
      huddled in the
      string-quartet close
      to her deeply
      sighing symphonies,
      exhaling evening in
      the fall to the pillow
      did you ever imagine
      Stalin's five-year plan
      banning the avant-garde?

At the boy's conservatory
did you imagine then,
the inhaled years
of your life
would leave you
in armfuls of song,
sailing upwards
towards me, to this
unknown future? The warmth
of your Fifth Symphony
drawn in history,
crystalline, classic?

Teaching at Leningrad:
your Seventh
born amidst World War I
shedding youth
by the millions, crying
out for lullabies,

humming them
in bloody pits—
do you hear me
calling to you?
A century laid
on tear-stained pillows
wrapped in the Eighth's
Cold War, a fall
from grace, oboes
trilling demure:

Announcing death
in the Fourteenth
fearing no communist,
no government
meeting compositions,
kisses, eulogies—
I dance with you
in these emptied streets
do you hear me,
my voice raised?

Distant

As the faces the masks appear,
as I glance at the faces studying the masks
after "How Solemn As One By One"
(Washington City, 1865), Walt Whitman

How isolating as one by one,
As the screens flash white white and black, as faces scroll by where I lay,
As masks appear, I search for my own, studying the masks,
(As I glance upward from this screen studying you, dear user, wherever you are,)
How the thought of your tapping fingers to each post, desperate connections,
I see behind each post that scrolling a connected breath,
O the virus could never kill what we really are;
The Soul! Ourselves I see, breathe as one, masking one by one,
Waiting secure and separate from the virus that cannot reach
Nor death take, dear user.

About The Author

Sara Cahill Marron is the author of *Reasons for the Long Tu'm* (Broadstone Books, 2018) and Associate Editor of Beltway Poetry Quarterly. Her work has been published widely in literary magazines and journals such as *Gravel, Atlas + Alice, Joey & the Black Boots, Cordella, Newtown Literary, South Florida Poetry Journal, Golden Walkman, Lunch Ticket, Poetry in the Time of Coronavirus, New Verse News,* and others. You can read more of her work at www.saracahillmarron.com.

www.ingramcontent.com/pod-product-compliance
Lightning Source LLC
Chambersburg PA
CBHW021029090426
42738CB00007B/945